THE SMALL RESTAURANT OWNER'S GUIDE TO FINDING LOST PROFIT

The Small Restaurant Owner's Guide to Finding Lost Profit

Tara Stasi

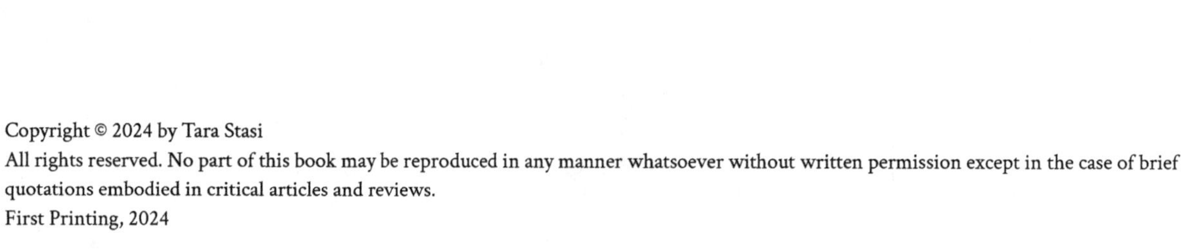

1

Introduction

If you remember only a few things about this guide when you're done, make it this:

- Nothing should be free. If you pay for it, your customers need to pay for it.
- You should know the cost of every single item in your inventory.
- Use the food cost calculator. Food cost percent is the cost of ingredients in a percentage compared to selling price.
- Arriving at an accurate, profit-making price includes: food/prep cost, packaging, all overhead, time, talent, and minor inventory increases.
- 30% is the bare minimum and not recommended. Labor heavy should be as low as 15%. This is typically for baked goods and breads where food cost is low and time to complete is high.
- For restaurant food service, 20%-25% will keep you in business with room to save for retirement. The lower the %, the higher the profit on ingredients.

Example: food cost for a big breakfast sandwich with thick bacon, 2 eggs, and cheese on a NYC bagel: $2.25.

Take $2.25/.30=$7.50. $7.50 is the bare minimum you should charge. This leaves no room for rising overhead costs and is not a price that will sustain your business.

But $2.25/.20=$11.25. That price gives the customer a big egg sandwich, and you a nice profit for the service/time/talent/overhead.

The loss of dimes turns into dollars. Thousands and thousands of them.

2

The Auditing Document Examples

Find me on my Instagram consulting business page @tarastasi to schedule a virtual or phone meeting to discuss your concerns, purchase the full documents, or schedule an audit of your small restaurant.

I can help you as little or as much as you need.

3

Unnecessary Services

Every business has different needs. For me, these were the things that I eliminated because they did not work for me to have them. The goal is for you to examine what you need and what you are wasting money on that is hurting your profit. If you are just building your business, refrain from paying for services until you know you need them.

1. **Food Distributor**: The minimum per order was $500. The problem was that they did not have everything I wanted or needed, including quality meats and cheeses. Their "thick" bacon was no better than grocery store bacon. I was ordering food I did not want or need due to the minimum and having to throw away vegetables that I could not use in time.

Savings: $500 per month plus food spoilage savings. I could now put that money towards inventory I actually wanted and used, and was now throwing virtually nothing away.

1. **Mat/kitchen towel service:** This was a $75/month, 5-year contract, and that contract term was cleverly hidden. I would never have signed a contract for that long because I was worried I wouldn't be in business for a full year. Restaurants' failure rates are high in the first year.

That said, I signed up for a service I did not need. As I mentioned in the beginning of this guide, this was one of the services that swooped in like a vulture. I needed this and it would help me, they said.

They delivered kitchen towels, kitchen mats, and entry rugs that had been chemically treated so often that they were breaking down and tattered. Corners were worn or curled up creating a tripping hazard, the black from the rubber stained my kitchen floors, and the towels were shredded with wear. This was not the quality they showed me when they wanted my business. Additionally, they would do their drop-off after hours, which was not in the agreement, subsequently leaving me with the load of dirty linens and mats from the previous month.

After 3 years I'd had enough, however, when I called, they quickly pointed me to the contract, where right there, outlined was a 5-year term. How did I not see that? They wanted $3,500 to buy it out. This was more than the per -month cost if I stayed for the remaining 2.5 years, which was what they wanted.

Now, back to the contract. I found clauses that outlined their promises for timely delivery and high quality, clean items, and these two items specifically were my focus, and had been from early on.

I typed a letter and sent it certified overnight, as per their requirement to potentially end the contract. I outlined the issues mentioned above, and I included many pictures. They immediately ended my contract with no buy-out required. Mention liability and the whole game changes.

Savings: $3,500 buyout/$2,250 for the remaining 2.5-year term. I purchased my own entry mats and disposable cloths. The total cost for those items over 1 year was $125 total.

* If this service is something you need, please do your profit a favor and check out the facility and items there. They bring show pieces for you to see that have never been used and it is not an accurate portrayal of the product you are paying for.

1. **Facebook Ads and Website:** The one thing I found is that clicks and likes on a Facebook ad mean nothing, and you must look at the data on your website to determine if the clicks may have generated business. You have to do research to determine which advertising is working for you so that you are not wasting hard-earned profit. What worked for me may not be the best advertising for you.

Regardless of the data Facebook shows you regarding your ad, you have no way of knowing if their ads generate any business for you. You choose your radius and demographics, but that guarantees nothing. There are people that will be included in your demographic that rarely open their Facebook, let alone bot/fake accounts.

I had other issues with Facebook ads as well:

1. I found that my non-paid non-tagged regular posts generated significantly more engagement than the paid ads. One in particular had over 80K views. I still don't know how; my followers were in the 2,500's.

2. People already following me who lived in the demographic are not my target audience. I really had no way of knowing if anyone who had not heard of my shop clicked on the ad. For all I knew, nobody new clicked on it.

3. I would see paid ads for other businesses on my personal page, read the comments, and I'd be shocked at how many people were angry that an ad they didn't want to see was on their feed. Yikes. I did not want to make someone angry with an ad to the point that they would not want to come in.

My website:

The issue with my website was that, based on the data I was utilizing in the back end, people from all over the world were clicking on my site. These are not organic clicks and these people happened upon my site searching for something else. The other issue was not having any way of knowing if clicks, organic or not, generated business.

Google ads:

I knew my Google ad was a great marketing investment because I had a call button enabled, so calls came in differently when customers used that. However, I still wanted to know if there were more that saw the Google ads but did not use the call button.

So, I started asking customers how they heard of my shop for one full year.

By and large, it was two things: word-of-mouth and my Google business page. Nobody mentioned the Facebook ads. Nobody mentioned my website. Both realizations made my stomach drop because I thought of all the money I'd wasted. Customers would subsequently follow me on my IG or FB business pages and see those FB ads, and from there check my website for my menu, but those were not the lead generators. On top of it, I already had my menu on both my Facebook and Google business pages. This pushed me to eliminate both the Facebook ads and my website as well. I gained precious time and money because I was no longer making edits across multiple platforms and paying to have them run. Fun fact: not one person ever asked where my website went.

Savings: $150 per Facebook ad two times per year running for 7-10 days each; $20 per month for the website, $275 every 2 years for website security and domain name.

1. **POS system that charged a monthly fee + passing the processing fees to customers:**
   - I had a system that not only took a cut of the credit card processing fee I paid, but they charged me $1,800 for equipment that was mediocre at best, and they charged $175 a month with zero added benefit. I was given a basic reporting feature and that was it. So, I shopped around and decided on NCR. Their processing fees were a little higher, but that's where they took their fee from. I had no monthly fee, the equipment cost me nothing, and the reporting features are second to none.
   - Pass the card processing fees to your customer and be aware of what each charges because they are all different. Remember, you cannot profit from this, and your transaction fees, usually 35-45 cents, are illegal to pass along. You must also post a sign informing customers of the exact charges you are passing to them. I also had "Cash Preferred" on that same sign which increased the cash customers used thereby decreasing my transaction fees each month.

Savings: Average $900 per month in processing fees; $175 per month/$2,100 per year in the monthly fee. Additionally, since you are passing the processing fees to the customer, you are only paying the transaction fees. Remember, you cannot pass transaction fees to customers and you cannot profit off the processing fees.

1. **Monthly accountant/Payroll service:** This one gets me. The need for a monthly accountant is dependent upon your business. I did not need one. What I needed was to do my own bookkeeping and then have an accountant do the tax season filing.

However, the most basic of things such as legitimate business expenses (health insurance, car insurance, mileage) he did not tell me about. I didn't start expensing those until the end of year two. Owning a business was new to me, so I had no idea. And I had no idea that I had no idea. For example, the fact that I was shopping my own inventory meant my car was primarily used for business. He never said, "You know, the insurance, mileage or fuel, maintenance, and any payment should be expensed." Same with my health insurance, home office creation to do work after hours, etc. It was mind boggling. What was I paying him for then? He wasn't helping me at all. I was sending all my expenses (already categorized) to him, so he was barely having to do bookkeeping. But he was happy to take the $330 a month plus the payroll service fee which was $75 a month.

After 2.5 years, I let him know I was disappointed with the service and why I no longer needed his service. I saw the official expense categories on the IRS site so I could do my own bookkeeping, and I purchased a payroll service for $52/month (plus $6 per employee) to do my own payroll. This service guided me to the tax websites to sign up for so their software could properly deduct taxes (UC, local, state, federal). On top of it, now that I was using the state portal, my monthly sales tax filing saw a 5% discount for filing online.

Savings: $330 per month/$3,960 per year in accounting fees; $23/month/$276 per year in payroll service fees

1. **Extra Wi-Fi line:** The bottom line was that I was not willing to continue paying $40 per month for other people to access the Internet. I ended that in my second year. Additionally, people sat for the entire day at the tables not allowing others to sit, have their sandwiches, and go about their day. Remember, as a counter-service sandwich shop, while there were people that hung out, most did not. To have people there for hours to use my Internet…that came a stop.

Savings: $480 plus taxes and surcharges

4

____

The Loss & Savings Breakdown

The information in this chapter will help you audit your business.

Another piece of your business you must absolutely know: your daily break-even. My daily break-even was \$252/day after I did all the eliminating and cost-savings. Prior to figuring everything out, it was almost \$1,000/per day. For my business, the latter number was an impossible goal.

I will break my losses down by outlining what I found during year one, year two, etc., the changes I made, the losses I incurred, and the savings, and the changes.

About my business: It was a New York style breakfast and lunch sandwich shop situated in a Victorian space I rehabbed. No burgers, salads, or the like, but my sandwiches were big and fresh with quality ingredients, made-to-order, and that's what I was known for. I did all the cooking. No need for help due to this being a smaller operation. It was a deli-style shop but with a little more flare, counter-service, no wait staff. Everything was disposable to keep things moving especially when it was busy. Customers threw their own trash out and I or my help cleaned the tables off. Very simple operation with an easy flow. I would often say it was a food truck with seating.

I utilized my point-of-sales system to audit operations on a number of levels once I realized not doing so was asking for failure.

The First Six Months

1. I changed my business hours and days.

- I went from being open 6:30 am – 2 p.m. to being open 8 am – 1 pm.
- I closed on Mondays.

Data showed I simply had few to no customers until after 8 am and business consistently slowed after 12:30 pm.

Data also showed Mondays were consistently slow, often with less than 10 customers. This meant every Monday for six months, I did not break even and I went into Tuesday mornings in the red. It sometimes took half a day to get into the black.

Labor cost savings (not including employer taxes): Staff was getting paid an average of $11 per hour plus tips. I had 4 staff members working each day. By changing my hours, I was saving $1,232 per month. By eliminating a poorly performing day at the original business hours, I was saving $1,320 per month. Over a 12 month period, that is a labor savings of $30,624.

Eliminating Mondays savings: Labor Savings: $1,320 per month, $15,840 over a 12 month period. Gas utility savings (griddle and oven use were always high): $25.33 per month, $304 over a 12 month period.

Utility savings:
Gas

- For some unknown reason, the oven was turned on from open to close the first six months. For a gas oven this is unnecessary because it heats up in no time. For my business, I was baking bagels to order, but not the entire business day. The griddle always had to be on, but it was always on low.
- Gas savings per month: The bill went from an average of $190 per month to an average of $85 per month.
- Gas savings per year: Average of $1,260

Electric

- Because of the changes, there was no reason to leave the heat or air conditioning on for 16 hours during non-business hours.
- When I closed for the day during the winter I'd put the heat on 62 and during the summer I'd put the air on 76. I would use fans to circulate the heat or a/c when I arrived in the mornings.
- Electric savings per month: The bill went from an average of $275 per month to an average of $130 per month.
- Electric savings per year: Average of $1,740

2. Analyze sales and reports.

Within 90 days, I began eliminating poorly performing menu items and replacing some with what ended up being very high performing items.

High quality meats and cheeses were being thrown away because people didn't want it. They were not feeling the salami or Fontina in particular.

I made very labor-heavy unique pastries, and it just was not something people wanted. They wanted homemade, but the area I was in had a community of people who liked simple, breakfast type goodies. I stuck to banana bread varieties, muffin varieties, seasonal items like pumpkin whoopie pies, apple fritter bread, etc. All of these simple items sold so fast I made multiple batches per week. The point? Check the sales data. You don't want to compromise your business model so it's more about shifting gears but staying true to your passion.

It is important to remember that you may want something to be available to customers, but if poor sales are telling you they don't want it, remove it.

I lost hundreds on the wasted food. I lost thousands on the profit of that tossed food.

But I profited immensely off the changes.

Year Two

1. Staff clocking in early and clocking out late.

I had 4 staff members. To make the math easy, let's say they were all clocking in 10 minutes early and then hanging out and clocking out 10 minutes later than the end of their shift. Each employee is now earning an additional 20 minutes of pay per day. Let's say they did this 4 days a week.

Cost savings: $235 per month, $2,819 per 12 months. This doesn't include employer taxes.

I started monitoring the clocking in and clocking out after discussing that as per the employee handbook, they may not clock in more than 5 minutes early or clock out 5 minutes late without permission.

That stopped the early in/late out very quickly.

2. I was overstaffed.

My business model was such that I didn't need all those people. I was lucky; some started not showing up, others were caught stealing. When they were eliminated I did not rehire. I also started doing all the cooking because it was not consistent. Good, consistent food is what keeps people coming back.

- I eliminated 3 staff members and kept 2 that each worked 3 days a week.
- This was the equivalent of 1 full-time employee.
- I saved $1,732 per month or $20,790 over a 12 month period.

3. I started auditing inventory and supplies. Make a point of auditing yours.

- **Dinner Napkins**

These were available for customers to take at will, some took a couple dozen for their cars and purses. This additional taking of napkins was not included in the menu item cost. Meals were served with two.

Over the course of one month in particular, I had 5,000 customers. That would be approximately 10,000 dinner napkins.

However, I went through 15,000 napkins. This meant that during that month, another 5,000 napkins were taken by customers or given to them to clean spills, and that cost was not included in the menu prices.

So here's the breakdown of the loss and what I did to turn it around:

A case of 3,000 ¼ fold 2-ply dinner napkins cost $47.16 with tax.

I purchased 5 cases that month, totaling $235.80.

Each napkin is .02; this means .04 was included in the selling price.

However, .06 total should have been included to cover the additional napkin per customer.

This means that for every meal sold, I lost not only the additional .02 per customer (the cost to buy more), but I lost the element of the food cost formula that would have added more for the time/fuel to get the cases each time.

Loss: Approximately $100 that month, $1200 every 12 months. This loss would increase during busy months.

Every dollar matters.

While not every customer took extra napkins, they were taken nonetheless.

I stopped leaving napkins out.

I stopped giving customers napkins to clean spills at tables and used reusable sanitized kitchen clothes instead.

I stopped buying the expensive, thick dinner napkins. I really only needed the lunch napkins. I owned a sandwich shop, not a plated meal restaurant.

I switched to 2 ply lunch napkins and continued to give 2 per person.

Each case contained 6,000 napkins at a cost of $48.21. I was getting double the napkins for essentially the same price.

I only purchased one case during the first month I implemented the changes. Some months I had to buy 2 cases because the customer count increased during the busy seasons.

Cost savings on napkins for a month with 5,000 customers: $188.64. For every 12 months, $2263.68 This number would be higher during months with a higher customer count. Ultimately, I was not buying nearly as many cases of napkins.

- **To-Go Bags**

I was using a bag for the single-item orders.

I stopped doing that, and not one customer cared. It's less waste, and less for them to deal with in their vehicles.

- 6 lb. bag cost was .03 each.
- The first month I stopped giving bags, I saved $12.
- Over the course of 12 months that is $144.

When you have so many items shrinking your profit, this seemingly small amount adds up, and it adds up quickly.

- **Butter**

This one kills me and it was a loss I was not expecting.

While I did start making my own butter in my third year of business, initially I was buying it. It was $3.89 a pound.

I was buying 12 pounds a week.

Aside from using it for my baked goods, customers would request griddling for their bagel, sandwich bread, or one of my homemade pastries.

I wasn't charging for it.

My thought was, "it's just a little bit."

It was just a little bit thousands of times.

It took me 2 full years to realize just how much butter I was going through and the money that I lost both in the butter cost and in the use of my griddle (gas), and my time at the griddle to prepare the food. Sometimes they'd want the butter on the side, so now I was giving away the portion cup and knife for free. I paid for all of that and made zero in return.

The butter alone? I lost $186.72 per month in purchase cost alone. I made no money for the cost of refrigerating the butter, using the butter, or my time and utility cost to griddle the food item.

Over the course of 12 months, I lost $2,240.64. And that did not include my time and fuel to get the butter, fridge storage, portion cup, or disposable knife.

I stopped giving butter (or any condiment) away for free. Customers didn't like it, but it was part of my livelihood. Why offer a service if it's going to be given away for free? People wanted ketchup, mustard, mayo, my homemade butter or homemade cream cheese, and other homemade sandwich spreads…for free. Unless it was already on the sandwich, it was not included in the selling price. If I put time into making it and I had to pay for the ingredients, they had to pay, too. I'm not sure when the mentality that the small things should be free started, but when they entered my shop and they wanted something that I had to buy, then they had to buy it, too.

- I started making my butter homemade and charging $1 per portion. The cost to make it was less; however, my time, expertise, ingredient cost, equipment usage cost, and cost to refrigerate all has a price.
- I started going through about 15 pounds of homemade butter a week once I advertised that it was now homemade.
- One $5 half gallon of heavy whipping cream made 8 pounds of butter.
- One portion of butter was 1 tablespoon.
- For every $5 half gallon, I could get 256 portions of butter.
- I was now rightfully earning $256 for every 8 pounds of butter. Per month, the earnings were approximately $2,048.

This is the way you stay in business.

- **Too Many Drink Choices**

I had 35 options. I realized something was wrong when I began having to throw away or give away drinks-by the dozens- that had reached their best-by dates.

They were big, unique, and priced right. What was the problem?

In my research to figure that out, I happened upon research that said if people have too many choices, it becomes overwhelming, and many will choose nothing.

So, I tested it out. Once I got rid of the drinks I could no longer serve, I looked at the reports of what sold. It was mostly the orange juice, apple juice, and water. But I needed more that just that. I chose a regular and diet soda, a chocolate drink, and I found a small business down south that made sweetened and unsweetened iced tea. I purchased a couple of small cases of each.

Each variety had three or four rows of 5 or 6. It was easy on the eyes, it was uncluttered, it was easy to see what was available, and, within a few days I sold more drinks than I had in a month.

- **Disposable cups**

People wanted cups of water. The cup costs me money, but customers cannot be charged for tap water.

- My first month in business, I went through 400 plastic cups for water. I didn't charge for a single one.
- Each cup cost was .08.
- I lost $32 giving cups filled with water away.
- Over the course of 12 months, I had lost $384.

Use glass cups you say? Well, you still have to purchase them, you still have to pay to run them through a high-temp dishwasher. You still have to pay for the soap and electricity. It's costing you one way or the other. If you use glass, then you have to raise menu prices to accommodate the cost of maintaining them.

This was yet another thing some customers didn't like. They don't expect these items for free when they go shopping for their own household, but you as a small business owner...some feel you owe them.

You don't.

While customers are the bread and butter of your business, there will be no business if you're afraid to rightfully charge for things that cost you money.

Year Three

I continued my audit of inventory and supplies.

- **Coffee cups and the self-serve station**

This one is multi-pronged.

Bigger cups mean more coffee per cup. More coffee per cup means you have to charge more and make coffee more often. More coffee means more creamer and sugar are used, and the cups themselves cost more. People don't like higher prices no matter how legitimate. I also noticed the larger 16 ounce cups of coffee were not being fully consumed. I switched to 12 ounce cups.

If you pay a premium for coffee, free refills should not be an option, and don't provide self-service like I did. We kept the cups and lids behind the counter, but found people would "top off", steal an entire cup the second you turn your back, or give their cup to a friend to steal a full cup. They are also adding sugar and creamer at your expense. You can have signs all over the place saying no topping off and refills are not free. It won't matter. If you're not careful, this seemingly benign loss will eat into your profit in no time.

What caused me to audit the coffee was that I knew how many cups a gallon of coffee would provide. I was making way more coffee than the number of cups I was selling. In the end, a full gallon--or more-- *per day* was being stolen. What was intended to be a convenience turned into a free-for-all at the expense of my profit.

- Cost for a 12 oz cup of coffee not including sugar, creamer, lid, cup, stirrer: I paid $22/lb. for single origin organic coffee.
- 1 lb. of coffee grounds made 5 gallons. That's $4.40 per gallon.
- 1 gallon of coffee makes 9-10 cups. It was costing me .44 cents per cup. I was making up to 3 gallons a day, depending on the day.
- Add in the sugar, individual creamers, etc.: my cost was .82 cents per cup. I was charging $3.75. I'm making less than $3 per cup.
- Deduct the half a gallon (5 cups) or full gallon (10 cups) per day that was being stolen, at a minimum.
- 30-60 people per week were getting free cups of coffee at my expense.
- This was both people who both didn't want to pay the $1.75 refill price or customers who shared their cup and stole a full-priced cup of coffee.
- Minimum I'm losing: $5,040 per year making a gallon more per day. That's just the refill price. If they stole a full cup: minimum $10,800 loss.

I moved the coffee to behind the counter, and the financial gain was noticeable after one month. I was now buying half the coffee I had been but still selling just as much. I also went from buying 3-4 boxes of 360 creamers per month to just 1 box. If only I had noticed this sooner. It was disheartening and upsetting. People took the coffee only thinking of themselves, never once thinking that they are one of thousands who stole from me each year.

You must control customers' access to your inventory. They will take, take, take and think nothing of it. And then when your business fails these same people will be shocked and not realize they were possibly the only reason why.

Be aware of where your profit is disappearing to.

- **More on the coffee...**

Shelf stable creamers went from $12 for 360 to $19 for 360 overnight. That's .04 cents per creamer to .06 cents per creamer. Only .02 cents you say? People pocket them. Some people use up to 10 creamers. That alone is .60 cents a cup that you may not have accounted for. Be aware of every cost all the time and make adjustments as necessary. Every penny matters.

- **Disposable cups/lids**
  - **Staff using new cups/lids/straws every time they wanted a new drink**

4 staff members using 4 new cups/lids/straws every time they got coffee, tea, or water (I didn't have a soda dispenser, so any bottled drinks were full price):

- Cup: .08 cents; lid: .02 cents; straw: .01 cent= .11 cents x 4(drinks)=.44 x 4(staff)=$1.76 So, $1.76 per day, 6 days a week all year= **$506.88**
- If you have a bigger staff, then your loss is bigger.
- Tell them to bring in a reusable cup or limit their cups to 1 per shift.

- **Disposable plates**
  - I used biodegradable sugar cane plates. They started out at .07 cents each.
  - During 2020, they shot up to .20 cents each which I had not realized for a full year. Not only was I not charging, but the increased price was not part of the formula for the selling price. I lost money in a number of ways on approximately twenty thousand plates. It would have up to five times as many, but during that year there was more to-go orders than stay orders.
  - In 2021, the price settled into $34.39 for 500 plates, or .09 cents each.
  - I had to increase my menu prices to accommodate that and other increases. But not before I lost a minimum of $2,600.

5

The Simple Takeaway

- Audit everything, often. Once you have done this a few times, item costs are something you'll notice every day without formally sitting down to figure it out.
- Know the price of every single thing you have in inventory and know when the prices go up.
- Know who is handling your money and account for every penny.
- Be at and work at your business every day.
- Knowing how to keep and increase your profit will save your business provided all other aspects are successful.

6

Profit & Loss Statement with Comparison

	A	Current Year	Q1 Q2 2024	Q1 Q2 2025	% Change (shown as +/- from current year)
1					
2	**Income**				
3	Income-Sales				
4	Income-Misc				
5	Income-Interest				
6					
7	**Total Income**				
8					
9	**COGS**				
10	Food/Drink				
11	Small Equipment/Furniture				
12	Supplies				
13	Wages Expense				
14					
15	**Total COGS**				
16					
17	**Gross Profit (income-COGS)**				
18					
19	**Expenses**				
20	Payroll Tax				
21	Payroll Processing				
22	Advertising				
23	Software				
24	Internet				
25	Utilities				
26	Office				
27	Repairs/Maintenance				
28	Auto				
29	Insurance				
30	Interest Expense				
31	Processing Fees				
32	Dues/Subscriptions				
33	Security				
34	Professional Fees				
35	Rent				
36	Uniforms				
37	Small Equipment				
38	Depreciation				
39					
40	**Total Expenses**				
41					
42	**Net Income (gross profit - total expenses)**				

7

The Shrinking Profit

I built, owned, and ran a highly successful sandwich shop for years.

I was not looking to sell, but a retired area pizza shop owner specifically wanted to own a sandwich shop that was already well-established with a good reputation.

He found my shop and made me an offer I could not refuse.

Now I provide business coaching based on my experiences, specifically where I lost money.

My coaching is two-fold:

1. To help small, independently owned restaurants avoid the financial mistakes I made, and

2. To help them stay in business if they are busy but seeing profit margins shrinking, but they have no idea where the money is going.

I know where it is going.

And I promise, in the end you will not understand how you never saw it in the first place.

Had I not caught the shrinking profits, even being at my shop 100% of the time and doing all the cooking, I'd have been out of business long before.

The simple math: By year six I'd had almost 600,000 customers. If every customer felt entitled to (and they do) even .20 cents of my inventory for free, that's $120,000 out of my pocket. And that's not including the tens of thousands of dollars in other losses owners do not see happening.

Owners must know every penny leaving their business.

When it comes specifically to losses incurred on account of customers, remember they are often helping themselves to and asking for items for free that you put time, fuel cost, storage cost, and ingredient cost into.

Your ass, your gas. But they think you owe them. This will be a recurring theme in this guide.

They don't think the chains stores owe them. They want a piece of the little guy.

By the beginning of year two, I'd had enough.

I'd had enough because I did the math. I'll show you exactly what I audited, what I found, and how much money I both lost and saved, so that you can do the same. This is something that can be turned around quickly and you will see a change within thirty days. At the end of the first year that you begin your audits and make necessary changes, we're talking anywhere from tens of thousands to hundreds of thousands of dollars, depending on your restaurant.

I continued to audit every single year, until I had squeezed out all the losses and my bank account grew instead of stagnated or decreased.

This guide does not cover every item I audited because the goal is to help you see that the loss is happening everywhere.

Not paying attention will put you under. If you have food people keep coming back for, then the problem of shrinking profit lies elsewhere.

I would have gone under, and not on account of my food. People loved my food. It would have been because I was not watching every literal dime that left my business.

8

Everyone's Got Their Hand in Your Wallet

From the moment I was getting the space prepared for opening, every day someone's hand was in my wallet.

They wanted my money, and they intentionally chose a time when things were high stress and downright overwhelming to pretend they wanted to lend a helping hand.

They know you are in a time crunch, and they know you have a lot going on. And like vultures, that's when they swoop in.

Just sign this contract.

It'll be ten legal-size pages long with an eight font. You're not going to read in its entirety, and it will likely lock you in for years along with a termination fee if you try to end it because you no longer need/want the service or if your business fails before the term is up.

In this guide, I will break down the math, provide the selling price formula, provide you with what I did to legitimately end one of my contracts early and avoid the $3,500 "buy out", and tell you what to start auditing.

My documents and formulas will require you to know the cost of every single item you have. You should know this even without the documents.

You can't make a profit without knowing the costs of absolutely everything and what goes into making it, storing it, and serving it.

So, who's after your money? A lot of companies and distributors.

The kitchen towel/uniform company.

The kitchen/entry mat company (monthly fee with a contract).

The food and/or beverage distributor. Minimums are required; will you use it all before it expires? In some cases, it's more cost efficient to run your own inventory.

The coffee roasters.

The advertisers. (Word-of-mouth and a Google Business page are your biggest advertisers.)

The accountant (more on this later…while some businesses need a year-round accountant, smaller businesses may not.) Many only need a tax-time accountant if they learn how to do their own bookkeeping and payroll. But the accountants will happily take your $350 a month plus payroll service fees and not tell you that. That's minimally $4,200 a year out of your pocket.)

The company that wants to clean your restaurant.

The customers that want you to buy their homemade goodies to sell in your business even if their goodies have nothing to do with what you are selling.

The requests for donations.

The requests for gift certificates for raffles.

The local club wants to sell you 20 lbs. of blueberries.

The knife salesperson.

The person that thinks they deserve a discount for ordering a lot.

And my personal favorite, the customer that calls you cheap because you won't give them something for free. How's that for irony.

Then there's the employees:

Staff taking bottled drinks out of inventory during every shift.

Staff using new cups/lids/straws every time they want a drink during their shift.

Staff eating more than their allotted free meal (stealing/not paying for extra food).

Staff clocking in more than ten minutes early and hanging out and clocking out ten or more minutes late.

Being over-staffed.

Staff stealing out of the register/till/safe.

And then there's the food and supplies:

Leaving napkins out for customers? They'll take twenty of them for their cars and purses. They don't like to hear that it's stealing, but it is. This can cost you hundreds if not thousands a year. You are not adding the cost of twenty napkins to each menu item, which means this is eating into your profit.

They need "a little" side of homemade cream cheese, homemade honey mustard, or even more mayo? You're putting in your time to make it or go buy it, paying for the portion cup, and the knife you're probably providing with it. Tens of thousands of times over the course of, let's say, every five years. The numbers will shock you.

Serving coffee on a self-serve buffet? They'll steal refills even if there's a sign that says refills are not free. It's "just" a top-off. They are also adding more sugar and creamer to the coffee they just stole. The loss on this will boggle your mind.

They'll also pocket the shelf-stable creamers.

Some customers think small business owners should expect this loss. I think this type of thinking is abominable and precisely why menu item costs are high and why small restaurants serving good food go under. I know customers think this way because I've been told by my own customers. It wasn't a cordial conversation, I'll tell you that.

The list can and does go on and on.

Knowing this information can and will save your business.

9

Other Financial Considerations

The list below contains suggestions that I personally experienced and implemented. **They can and will be game changers for your finances and your restaurant's success.**

1. If you have any extra money each month, put it in a high-yield savings (HYS) and/or set up automatic transfers for an amount you are comfortable with. It is what I did and earned hundreds a year in a risk-free account. Like any savings account, you can easily and quickly transfer money back and forth. HYS offers from 4%-6% depending on the bank you use, and it is significantly more than what regular savings accounts offer. Fidelity, American Express, and Capital One are just two that offer HYS.

2. Use your POS reporting system to analyze how your menu items are doing at least once per quarter. When items are failing, it means there is food waste. Either replace it or revamp/reintroduce it if you think it has potential.

3. Overlap your menu item ingredients. Nothing throws money away quicker than having an ingredient that is only used on one or two items.

4. Keep your menu on the smaller side. Nothing says "frozen food here" more than a menu with lots of pages. Focus, specialize, and have a niche that no one in your area has. My sandwich shop was New York style, and some thought I should have pancakes/waffles/plated meals. Nope. There were nine diner-style eateries within walking distance of my shop. No community can sustain sharing customers among almost a dozen of the same type of place. On top of it, I had no desire to cook diner food. The result? My specialty focus is specifically what people came in for, and thousands had said over the years "I can't get this anywhere else in the area". That's the exact sentiment any business owner wants to hear.

10

Food Cost/Selling Price Formula

Refer to Chapter 1 if you need a refresher on this formula.
Be sure you are pricing for the exact amount of ingredients you are using for your menu items. This is the only way to make a profit.

	A	B	C	D	E	F	G	H	I	J
		Cost/pkg	Cost/lb	Cost/oz	Cost/Bottle	Cost/Each	Total Ingredient Cost	TOTAL FOOD Cost/25%	DRINK COST/50%	Selling Price (ROUND UP)
2	Pastrami		7.79	0.49			4 oz/sandwich=1.96			
3	Swiss	3.29 (10)				0.32	2/sandwich=.64			
4	Lettuce	2.29 (15)				0.15	2/sandwich=.30			
5	Tomato (10 slices/tomato)	3.29 (5)				0.65/tomato; .07/slice	4 slices/sandwich=.28			
6										
7	Gingerale	37.99 (24)			1.58				3.16	3.75
8	Iced Tea	33.37 (12)			2.75				5.56	3.95
9	Chocolate Milk	25.85 (24)			1.08				2.15	3.95
10										
11	Straws	15.55 (1000)				0.01				
12	Cups	67.55 (1000)				0.07				
13	Napkins	50.55 (3000)				0.02				
14										
15	Menu Item 1						3.55	14.2		14.25
16	Menu Item 2						1.72	6.88		7.25
17	Menu Item 3						2.66	10.64		11
18										

11

Inventory Excel Sheet

I used this to keep track of all inventory and prices, even drilling down to cost per slice, etc. This helped with both the selling price formula and also keeping track of rising costs and adjusting menu item pricing.

	A	B	C	D	E
2	**Coffee Items**				
3	Alpha	82		.40/cup (all)	.40/12 oz
4	Sugar	RS	25 lb bag	$14.27	.04/oz
5	Sugar in the Raw	Walmart	3 lb bags	$6.98	
6	Half & Half	RS	1 box	$15.29	.04 each
7				**$36.54**	
8	**Drinks**				
9	Water	Walmart	32 16.9 oz bottles	$6.69	$0.21
10	Pepsi/Diet 12 oz bottles	Pepsi	6/12 oz	$3.66	$0.61
11	Assorted teas	Harney	50 bags	$11.22	.22/bag
12	Hot Chocolate	gourmet		$1.40	$1.40
13	Assorted Tea Bags	gourmet		$0.75	$0.75
14					
15	**Meats**				
16	Bologna Patty	RD		5.72/lb	1.07/3 oz
17	Bacon	RD			.66 per piece
18	Taylor Pork Roll	RD	2 96 oz rolls	107.90 (w/shp)	.78/piece
19	Corned	JG		7.29/lb	.46/oz
20	Ham	JG			.49 per slice
21	Tky	JG		$5.23	0.32

12

Expenses Worksheet

The IRS website has exact expense categories. For example, my ADT line item would actually be under "securities expense" when tax season rolls around.

	A	B	C	D	E	F	G	H	I	J	K	L	M
1		January	February	March	April	May	June	July	August	September	October	November	December
2	Accounting/Payroll Service												
3	ADT												
4	Advertising												
5	Business/Home Internet												
6	CC Fees												
7	Computer/Accessories												
8	Dues/Subscriptions												
9	Equipment Maintainence												
10	Fuel												
11	Insurance												
12	Auto												
13	Inventory												
14	Lease												
15	Licenses, Permits												
16	Loan Interest												
17	Mobile Phone												
18	Postage												
19	Retirement/savings												
20	Salaries-Employee												
21	Salary-Owner												
22	Owner Draw												
23	Taxes-Payroll												
24	Uniforms												

www.ingramcontent.com/pod-product-compliance
Lightning Source LLC
Chambersburg PA
CBHW082041150726
47996CB00016B/3243